The Geographic Cure
Poems by Ellen Dudley

Four Way Books
New York City

Distributed by
University Press of New England
Hanover and London

Editorial Office
Four Way Books
POB 535, Village Station
New York, NY 10014
www.fourwaybooks.com

Library of Congress Catalogue Card Number: 2005928315

ISBN: 978-1-884800-74-0

Cover art: *Torrey Pines Afternoon, Del Mar, CA,* oil on paper, 22" x 30", ©2005, M. Portnow.

Cover design: K. C. Witherell/Hello Studio.

This book is manufactured in the United States of America and printed on acid-free paper.

Four Way Books is a not-for-profit literary press. We are grateful for the assistance we receive from individual donors, public arts agencies, and private foundations.

This publication is made possible with public funds from the National Endowment for the Arts and from the New York State Council on the Arts, a state agency.

Distributed by University Press of New England
One Court Street, Lebanon, NH 03766

[clmp]
We are a proud member of the Council of Literary Magazines and Presses.

ACKNOWLEDGMENTS

A number of the poems in this book have appeared in the following print journals and e-zines:

Agni Review: "Night Fishing"
The Adirondack Review: "Letter from the Road,"
            "The Road from Corpus Christi to Sangre de Cristo"
Alaska Quarterly Review: "Solfeggio"
The Alembic: "Equinox, New York,"
            "Call to Watch Hill—Crows & Rain"
The Best of Writers at Work, 1995: "The Bats"
canwehaveourballback: "Angel Gear," "Equinox"
Hunger Mountain: "Solstice," "Peak"
Isle Review: "Tyele-Koula"
The Laurel Review: "Lō`ihi"
Many Mountains Moving: "The Ojo Caliente Suite," "Kilauea"
The Massachusetts Review: "New Hampshire"
Sou'wester: "The Gator Pond Café," "Leaving Lincoln"

Thanks to the Vermont Council on the Arts for an Individual Artist's Fellowship and to Dorland Mountain Arts Colony, the Vermont Studio Center, Ann Stokes, and John and Elaine Mandas at the Kona Tiki for their gifts of time and space that allowed me to work on this book.

A deep gratitude to R. Irvine Hippert, R. Anderson Barnett, H. Fremont, M. Kaufman, J. Aleshire, & M. Rhodes, touchstones.

For ACG

Contents

The Bats

Just at dusk, when the man I lived with
had set about his drinking, wine glass polished,
ashtray on the couch arm, book in hand —
my daughter and I walked the quarter mile
to the dirt road, and at the top of the hill,
sun falling between the mountains in front of us,
she taught me how to call the bats, clicking
high-pitched in our throats.
                              And as the sky
gathered itself into a dark blue and Venus
winked like a plane's starboard wing tip, they came.
And whirring softly, they dived through our hair,
leaving us laughing with their wind on our scalps.
We stayed in the road until full-dark
when we picked our way back to the house,
which, lighted and open, looked like a refuge.

I

Tyele-Koula

In Sarajevo, a woman lies across her front stoop,
onions and potatoes spilling from a string bag
down her flowered skirt, and at her throat
a wound like a red poppy.

And I go back to the place between Belgrade and Niš,
where, among the minarets and saints,
I found the man in my compartment.

We had no common language and we didn't even kiss,
but I straddled him in the train car,
Sobranie in one hand, smoke
making halos of our heads in the sun,

and pink with the heat of slivovitz and sex, we passed
the remnants of the monument the Turks put up —
a high tower of Serbian heads — and there,

the hellish smell of soft coal in the air,
I rode him into the city Ptolemy mentioned in his writings
both of us panting, jerking with the train

till all we knew of outside was the green rushing past,
yellow humps of hills, the way the low sun
turned our skins crimson.

SHENANDOAH VALLEY, VIRGINIA

The moon lay in Taurus, sign of earth and sweat, as you went over the mountain where wind and altitude dropped the temp fifteen degrees, a minute's respite till back down in the valley, the humid world, where, when you moved your head, the hand resting on the headrest grabbed your hair and a charge arced so hard you put both hands on the wheel.

Your body rose from the seat slow and steamy in the heat, letting the wind hit your back as those fingers found your neck, thigh, and blood pooled in your belly, skin sang and every truck became a hazard and a joy. Leaning into that hand, hair rising from the car window like a flag, roar of a truck's slipstream and the blood in your ears like surf, you cut a swath through the end of the valley, sun low behind the trees turning your thigh a color from the crayon box: burnt umber raw siena — and on the stereo Robert Johnson's "That's All Right Mama."

Remember the dollar you saved out from the pooling of your money from that night's meal? Tucked in your wallet between the passport and a Feynman quote, you kept it as a talisman of the beloved body: from the lover's pocket to yours, imagined scent still clinging from a time you knew you'd never forget, until some Saturday morning downtown, going for pastry or a part for the lawnmower, you search out the two one dollar bills you have, and pay.

Or now, cleaning the house, you throw away junk, a tile from July 1969 — Neil Armstrong's boot print, photos, pennies, the broken umbrella from the weekend twenty years ago, a thing you kept as a memento of a name and face you can't remember now, the only flash remaining a shine of shoulder in the morning drizzle.

Angel Gear

Welcome to Eden the sign by the Catholic church reads
in a script so green and Bavarian I expect men in lederhosen
to cross the road, knees freezing in this place.
I'm singing *Summertime* and Gershwin bangs off the headliner
and slithers down the windows. Summertime — something
they don't have here — June rains, August frost.
If I kept on this road, I'd come to Canada. And at the border,
I'd think: *If I kept on this road...*

By the time I crest the hill, the song
is German and part of the air I'm taking in
is blow-by from the tank truck in front of me,
his road dirt on my windshield.
I get closer, try to see his plates, where he's from.
They're blue and white, *Je me souviens,* Québec.
He's going home, over the top and in angel gear
down the spine of these Green Mountains, held back by prayer
and his own weight.

I don't follow him, but turn back
toward the place that is not home, where I'll strike
an attitude against the wall and you'll get me down forever
on canvas — in color.
Then we'll lie on the rough wool blanket on the hard wood floor,
the smell of turpentine thick around us. And as the light goes,
I'll open my arms and you'll move into me
slow as a boat entering its slip.

DAKOTA

"...intimacy's repeated little shames..." —Rilke

Here, out past Grand Island comes the West;
the patchwork of farms left behind, and in that loom and stretch
of grassland — sedimentary rock that was once an ocean bed —
I begin to climb into the high plains.

I stop and, in a rest area, stand in the sprinkler's range
until I am doused, all the tender skin exposed
through my now transparent clothes and even a busload
of strangers doesn't shame me, nor does driving between towns,
after dark, shirt off, breasts flickering white in street
or truck lights and the guardrails singing by too close
because my hands have left the wheel.

And what is it I want from the purple Kenworth roaring
down beside my little car, not the small creature up there
enclosed, but some wild, imagined thing conjured by speed
and by the light cracking across the sky like a direction finder.

I remember turning away from a lover in the light, from the pill
bottle with his name on it, the socks hanging on the towel rod,
turning from him, when as he undressed, I saw a tiny fleck
of paper nestled beneath the pouch of scrotum. I wanted only
to dig my hands into the wool, taste buckle, denim, semen —
wanted to let him move my blood with his tongue, to take
him into me until we knew no boundary of skin or language.

Give me the body in the dark, the slick arc of cock sliding
up the thigh, teeth in the tender skin of armpit.
This is where I want to be let in — to this body,
which, even up against me, still hovers, is imperfect, and will die.

Leaving Lincoln

Stopping for gas on my way out of town:
the late wind blowing the poplar tops to ground,
tornadoes threatening from the south, I waited,
hipsprung at the counter. In front of me stood a shirtless
man and the dust of a day's work lined his smooth back
just above his jeans. And below his left ear three
gray hairs nestled in the black. Fresh from the library
where I'd held a dead man's poems all afternoon, I
was streaked with graphite from the pages where he'd
left his thumb print, and my own fingers shook a little.
What I wanted to do then, as the wind rattled
the roof, was to put my top incisors on that peak
of shoulder, let my tongue out to taste each grain
of salt, to feel the water molecules laid on by
the Nebraska afternoon.

THE GATOR POND CAFÉ

Leaving Georgia we cross the state line into central time
and the sun hangs like a ripe tomato over
the alfalfa fields and metal roofs. Birmingham,
Tuscaloosa — names loaded with Bull Connor
dogs and fire hoses — and in the morning
the sky a blue filled with water while bottom
fog settles over the fields and creeks south
of Jackson and a Volkswagen lies against a thick pine,
its roof wrapped around the trunk like ribbon.

We cross the big river at Baton Rouge
as it moves brown and sluggish towards
New Orleans, and Lake Charles lies deserted in the rain
but for the long Chevy outside the café
where we come out arm in arm and laughing
and the four men in the car stare and shift.

They watch two women, speculate lovers because
we are easy with each other. I could tell
them, lean into the car window and tell them:
were I to choose, I'd choose even them,
take them as I'd been taken, their strange
other bodies, their hair in my teeth, sweating
over their man-smell, their utter difference.

THE ROAD FROM CORPUS CHRISTI TO SANGRE DE CRISTO

Outside Seguin, a billboard says you can hunt year round
— in safety — and the Army boys love it.
They gather the way the Navy boys gathered in my living room
where I brought beer, wore shorts against my husband's edicts,
stayed across the counter while they watched the movie:
a naked man bent over a blonde woman on her hands and knees,
the veins on his arms and neck standing out
as he held her shoulders, her throat, rammed at her
until she wasn't pretending, until her eyes widened
with surprise, then fear, and she was thrashing
and the only sound you could hear was his breathing, her choking
until his harsh wail covered everything in my house
and she didn't move anymore. The tail of the eight millimeter
reel slapped the projector and nobody said anything —
just like I don't say anything now years later, driving across
the Pecos, left foot up on the dash to catch the wind, long tan
expanse of thigh exposed, as a trucker passing hisses his
air-brakes and swerves. I don't even give him the finger.
But I think about the way two thumbs on the temples
held my head steady while that tongue traced a line
from ear to clavicle, palms on my carotids.
I remember the Beretta between us, its blue heft warming
on my belly, my hand resting on its grip, as a man
whose name I can't recall moved in me.
Out here now, the night is coming on, and when the moon rises
full and burning, I'll kill the lights and ride the shining
white line into the desert dark.

THE OJO CALIENTE SUITE

The Oranges

It has been days since I sat with you
as you pulled the little dagger
from your pocket and cut around the fruit until
it gave off its rind in spirals, and I'm still full
of the smell of you, your heady slipstream —
full of the sight of you sinking into me.
You sliced right through the navel and juice poured
out over the blade and even now I want to draw its edge
across my tongue.
          Here at my kitchen sink, I jam
my thumb in by the stem, pull the peel
in clumps, and with the liquid running down
my wrists and chin, the whole room reeks
of blood orange, tangelo, mineola
and I see in my reflection at the kitchen window
that the three small bruises on my neck —
where you held on as I bore down —
have faded to a smudge.

Recall

To keep myself from this lover, to shut the door,
I clean the bathtub. Stinking of chlorine,
I close the curtain, a varicolored
children's map, and there under my left hand

is home to him, time zones away — so
I drive the fire truck because I know
the concentration it will take. And wheeling
the big Reo diesel through the back roads,

the fields green enough this spring
to set your teeth on edge, I try to find the place
low range kicks in, the torque just right.
Shifting on the curves, the muscle memory is back,

the gears come easy now and I know
forgetting is the last thing the body does.

Corporeal

This morning, I found I could say your name clearly,
without sound, in the back of my throat —
no labials in that one syllable,
but a secret I could keep — over and over
as he moved on me, against me;
when I put my arms around him I took your name
in my mouth, in quiet, the way
prisoners learn to come silently in the cell,
the bunk barely moving, the air
undisturbed around them while the earthquake
takes place in the throat, the gut,
the dry heart.

Hot Eyes

As you lifted off, I drove, windows open,
deep into the Sangre de Cristo.
While you changed planes in Denver, I came over
the top of the pass into Colorado and for a minute
we were in the same state again.

A town called Angel Fire to the east,
west the hostile teeth of the Rockies,
and my hands sliding on the wheel wafted
the scent of the night's semen. The red dirt
pinged in my wheel wells — Colorado,
red in Spanish, that sweet redolent tongue —
red, the color I left last night
on your rented bed.

Now you're sleek over the Marin Headlands,
the Pacific booming, beckoning you.
I'm heading east, your gaze still on me like a hand.
Seventeen time zones and I still believe
we could wake to bananas and passion fruit,
that my brown skin will wear a sheen of sweat
and when you touch me you will shake fire
from your fingers. In the humid room,
under the net at night, you will slide
your palm up my slick thigh; my mouth
will groan *no* and my body rise to you.

Bon Voyage

Now that you are leaving, let me tell you what I love:

To fish — whistling the line to the middle of the stream —
and all that time to think

The curve of my own lip

Oysters

Any song by Hugo Wolf

A freighter passing westbound through the Golden Gate

Wind from the southeast

The feel of raw silk

And rain on your mouth.

PHILADELPHIA

In a hotel room on the seventh floor
he's dozing after sex and the woman's
in the shower singing a song by

Hugo Wolf — a prayer that culminates
in a high B-flat and slides down startling
him awake and anxious. Still in-country

twenty-five years hence, he sweats awake
to this strange room smelling of sandalwood
and sex. In the night, in fear, he had

placed his hand on her belly, aorta in
there pumping faintly, and calmed,
went back to sleep.

In his wallet, on the dresser by the door
of this room far from her husband, his
wife, a grainy snapshot he carries

always: three men in fatigue pants
and boots. Even now the tall one looks
like him, huge and pelted ... laughing

and terrified as he was for that whole
year there, he stands beneath a palm,
beer in one hand, M-16 in the other.

At six foot six he is more than twice
her weight and when he wakes screaming,
she is reminded of the horses of her

childhood, tries to recall how to
comfort something, someone
who multiplies her size. She speaks

low and slowly, puts her hand
on him — tone alone keeps him from
bolting — and he breathes, and thanks
her, and sleeps.

THE ONE THING

Then I waited on a park bench in Athens,
outside the agora, for a man in cotton pants,
black-haired and beautiful. And there in the rain
under the garden Priapus, I opened my coat
to give breasts, belly, thighs to a loving tongue.
Now it's another April light, and cold,
and I'm putting this on the table for you.
And with every hiss and thump of consonant,
every mouthful of vowel — even though there are
no statues here, no plane trees muttering *Never
be importunate, ephebe* — I open my coat.
Here, I say, *Taste.*

II

The Coriolis Effect

Just at dusk, in Detroit as the streetlights come on,
the cop takes aim, and though he couldn't tell
you why, corrects a little to the west
and hits the kid — dead center — in the back.
And the delicate shower looks yellow in the sodium vapor.

At Key West, on this warm April night, a man
explains the perfect wave — ebbing tide
and following sea — as the woman makes
wave a note, surfing on the top of a high B-flat,
trying to find the common in wave, pitch.
She says his name, a spondee, simple as a hinge,
as eyes across a room, the easy way desire
arcs across space and makes the throat thick,
joints like water. He needs to inhabit her bones;
she wants his skin her own. They kiss. The earth spins on.

In Rio, the Guardia Captain gets the six-year-old thief,
watches the blood sluice from under the striped jersey
and puddle in the flat street. At the station,
he sucks in his gut, shakes himself over the toilet,
watches idly as the cigarette butt spins round and round,
then buttons his fly — and calls it a day.

ARIZONA

Signify, the license plate reads and I think
the car must belong to a semiotician
or a soul singer — those old songs where the singer
testified his love and signified by action:
I don't care if you don't want me, I'm yours.
And from the radio no melody but a hard bass line
entering through ears and skin straight to the gut
and for a minute, I'm lost, gone from the street
to no place or time that *was*
but something made by memory.

Or weeks ago, as evening came on the wind blew
the smell of wet creosote and the Pacific in
from the west and the black rags of cloud gathered
over the Huachucas and for a moment the woman in
the Hopi-print blouse ceased to be Nelda from east Texas.
I could tell by inflection that her speech was English but
did not hear it. And I didn't try, the way you sometimes
try to strain to hear a conversation at the next table
because the tone says you want to know *what happened.*

Her shirt ceased to be green and red and white
but instead was a cliff in spring, just as
the first green comes against the harsh sky.
And I was out of body — as I feel now in the rest
area near Acoma, the sun crashing down on a world
where the two men in the orange highway truck are whistling
at a woman in a black silk shirt and cowboy boots
she bought a year ago in El Paso, the ones I never clean
because I like the dust of Casa Grande, Blythe, Las Cruces,
the dust of times I cannot separate, covering them.

Equinox

That morning as I left you in the half-light,
you stood in the hall, body sloping and no longer
young, but filling me with want like hot wires.
And no matter what fiction I make of this later,
I did not run my fingernail down your midline,
sternum to pubis, did not gather your genitals
in my hand like a bunch of grapes, sweet and edible,
did not let out my tongue to do any damage.

I kissed the mole next to your left nipple and you
breathed into my hair. Your cock coated with my juices,
bright bits of you swam in me; swimming the distance
from here to Senegal, poor brainless things. Weeks later
I think of those swimmers now making their way past
Cape Verde, imagine my smell still on your hands
and when you raise them to eat or shave,
your pulse stutters.

You deep in me, the swimmers, even these words
won't last. Yet, for seconds back there in the night,
we became nothing. Nothing on that bed but melting bones,
a bundle of light.

SHADOWS

Hairline receding, voice high and sure as it was twenty years ago in front of thousands, the folk singer is playing the gym tonight. Now it's bars, town halls, high schools in rural nowhere. By a sign for his performance tacked to a phone pole, two men idle in a beat-up Chevy truck with temporary plates. December sixth, almost Christmas. Two fishing poles lie in the gun rack at the back window, and in the gray glare of the near solstice the leaders are dancing in the light. There's no fishing now; even the moving rivers are black with a scrim of ice, and in this just-acquired truck with its new plates, the rods are there for April as the year spins down.

I remember walking the rocks at La Jolla where I put a message in a bottle and sent it south to a lover I never hoped to see again although I could all but feel those shoulders in my hands, taste the wet wool I sunk my face and fingers into. And on the rocks, the carved names: *Denise, Randy, Lisa, Chuck*, hearts and the word *forever* being spattered by the afternoon's tide. Out there the seals labored on and off a rock covered, then uncovered by the sea.

I was an artist's model once, an artist who wanted his subjects against the wall, light overhead so I had no shadow, not distinct but part of a *greater whole*. That was years before the red-haired woman in the bar who strung curses in melismas and cracked a beer bottle against the bathroom sink, watched the way my little knife opened the underside of her arm, yellow and red, fat and blood rising, like a spring pond, gentle and slow it seemed, before she could punch the ragged glass through my carotid. All this over a man who, dead by now, didn't care.

Her arm, my neck, scars fading to fine lines and the singer with sparse blond hair combed straight back, the bus crossing the freezing rivers out of this frozen town to another like it and the artist in a studio somewhere covering the canvas with red and yellow in the gunmetal light of year's end.

And here, as the traffic light turns green, the truck bucks a little, the driver with his new clutch — and as the first flakes begin to spiral down, glare hits the window, the fishing lines disappear and the lures spin as if levitated, weightless in the late light.

TROY

In this backwater town where the hill runs down
to the river, not far from the boarded-up triple deckers,
a man stands outside the back door of a sandwich
shop and we can hear him across three lanes where we
sit at the light. The young girl in front of him, blonde
and small, looks at his face then down at the cup
she sips from, as he, arm cocked, hand on hip,
gestures with the other hand. He's open to her,
belly pressing the untucked blue shirt, planted legs,
the body aggressive and what we hear across three
lanes is: *That's* my decision, then That's *my* decision!
Over and over, his mantra and we can wonder if
he berates his wife like that, or even if he has one,
or what he goes home to and when. The girl, young,
neat, uniformed and pretty, doesn't flinch. Does he
think he's humiliating her, out here where the whole
neighborhood can hear? And when the light changes,
and we drive west to Albany, and blessedly past,
that picture won't go. Power is so fluid. What she
has is youth and he has her, or thinks he has. A
man. A boss. And sure as any of the rest of us to
die. What does he gain? What does he gain by this?

West Virginia

It's night, evening really, and what we hear
between the hills is music from the windows —
harmonica, pennywhistle and from outside,
the snapping of the fire and the low rumble
of men's voices under these stars
of Pochahontas county, WVA.
It could be some other year, year of war
a century and a half past and the voices   .
those of soldiers camped along the Gauley
or Potomac. It could be some other soft
September night and the strains of *Shenandoah*
on fiddle or harp, bespeaking
possibility of home and future.

Here on this property and those around it,
in the hollows, on the hillsides, the cousins
gather to celebrate the life of father, uncle. And
in this group and in this ground are those who
came from either side. The camp
might be blue or gray where they
are quiet by the fire, murmuring, the music
low. Come morning we all go on,
north or south, New England, Ohio,
Virginia, Carolina, our bellies full of
our host's corn bread, sausage and beans.

The bears wait out in the dark
and will come down to feed
when we're all still. And in the music,
the voices of the men around our fire, the boys
in blue or gray around their fire, and on the pipes
Amazing Grace, a pure strain that will raise
the hair on the neck and arms. And then
come morning, the ground a dust of frost,
apples dropping and deer stepping from

the deep fog to cross the road where the dam
forms the Gauley, one by one, we go, each pair
of taillights fading till they all are lost.

Carnifex

Here the largest earthen dam in the east
looms over the rafters down on the Gauley,
(*the meanest piece of white water east of
the Mississippi*) and out the overflow
gates and pipes the water roars — sitting
on the bench below, you can imagine
the whole thing letting go, taking you with it
down the river, imagine just how quick
and awful that death would be.

We have walked the battlefield,
looked to the river below
where the soldiers forded, then climbed
this nasty hill to kill each other. And we
sit on this bench where the old man
pontificated on the state of this dam
and others like it. One day it *would*
let go. But not for him. What killed
him, melanoma, all those hatless
years of farming. And we, his daughter
and I, are of an age when everything seems
to die amongst us.

We imagine the soldiers, all the ghosts
who walk here. And now among them,
someone we know. Just last week,
returning my bottles to the redemption
center, I saw a man I knew
get out of the car beside me. That man
was two years dead, yet I began
to roll my window down to yell "Hello."

Isn't that the way of memory?
My hand on the crank, my friend's
father in another bald man

near the dam. So many people
who look just like the dead: walking,
sitting, buying wine, locking the car —
all of them, among us and around us.
They are who we see, the mind's
file has not yet consigned them
to the place they belong and so
they remain here with us
till time allows them to go.

Texas

Il pleure dans mon coeur
Comme il pleut sur la ville.
—Paul Verlaine, set by Claude Debussy

It's raining again in the hill country and the nutria
have flopped into the pond where, deep, it's warmer,
leaving their berry-stained scat on the dock, under
the hills, limestone buttes across the near horizon.
And out on the grass they'll burn next month,
out past the green Nueces river, the kestrel tacks
back and forth, her vision infrared and tracking
voles and their faultless trails of urine,
their perpetual incontinence giving away their spot
in the food chain.

And the boom of the rifle across the valley
startles the deer, though it won't be
their turn till next month when the men come
to cull the herd, tossing corn out and waiting
on the old car seat to plug the right one,
the tough old buck perhaps, at the end
of his breeding, hide scarred but antlers
like a hat rack. Fish in a barrel, these deer.

The oak and sycamore are going yellow
and the wind whips their branches down.
It's forty-six degrees and the meadowlarks
have quit their song for another year.
We'll come back in spring to see two oaks
dropped and the new deer grazing, the burned
fields sprouting native grass and the nutria,
ugly water rat, sunning itself, oblivious.

Elk

In Dakota, elk outnumber people almost two to one,
factoid of the day. Here on this Montana plain
the males approach each other, sidle up,
dipping heads and rolling muscled shoulders
like weight lifters. They paw the ground and the grazing
yearlings scatter as one female turns her back

to them, twitches her tail and saunters toward the trees.
The males see none of it, not trees, nor the walking
rain to the south. They don't even sniff the newly
wakened grizzly slapping trout from the river. They
are intent — on each other, on the circle of spoor one
calls home and the other covets, the trees, females, last

year's young. The racks, their antlers, are the things that
east coast men come to cull each fall. Leaving carcasses
to rot, they take the head, or solely
these antlers covered with elk velvet, that periosteum
of blood we carry on our own bones. Velvet peels
off on trees as new comes in, or sometimes

from each other, as now when the rack of one meshes
with the other's and there's a crack that reverberates
down the valley, and as they clack again,
the meadow echoes with a noise that sounds like *Mine.*

LETTER FROM THE ROAD

Yesterday, from the bridge over the summer trickle
of the Rio Grande, I watched a man who looked
like you play with his little son, and when the boy
opened his mouth, the whole arroyo filled with laughter.

Just across that river, in the Peace Park, Park
of International Understanding, they've found
the bodies of the Mexican whores, mummified,
baked black, faces frozen in a rictus that might
seem a smile. Girls, from Sonora, Chihuahua,
and south, stabbed and beaten and left by the smelly
river where the Maquilladoras dump T3E, benzine,
cadmium that floats toward Brownsville and the gulf.

And the girls who work the day shift pass
the park quickly at evening as the semis
lumber north across the bridge, the river,
carrying what we'll pay for back to us.

CALL TO WATCH HILL — CROWS & RAIN
in memory of Glenn Parker

Up at 6 a.m. in this strange place
and hiking to a campground phone to find
what I already know is true — with dread,

face pressed against the booth's glass wall, "He's dead,"
a voice across eight thousand miles of wire,
cable, satellite, through air, and my face

in the glass doesn't crumble where I trace
the word from the receiver and I'm blind
to crows and rain — as their noise crowds my head.

The Most Dangerous Profession

The contrail I've been watching disappear
is right over my head just now and I can
hear the distant roar passing the last land
for a while, out of Boston, across the bay,

over this spit of land where you can dig,
find wrecked timbers and the dust of
sailors. That town there, just ten years
past lost a dozen when the Captain Bill went

down with all hands. Fishing in November,
the crew's hands are red as beefsteak
as they unload the catch at the dock and lucky.
Lucky to get here. And hours later in the bed,

body to body but still bone cold and grateful to be
once again here, on land, home. And those
of us passing through, those at thirty thousand
feet, can see only the miles of blue-black

nothing they inhabit, fishing and looking,
always west, toward home.

SOLFEGGIO

You can solfege the foghorns here and the fog
is so thick it passes through an outstretched hand.
Just now a trawler chugged close to shore, the red buoy
somewhere off her port bow, through the channel
you could swim across if the water was more
than fifty-two degrees, and it isn't. The horns
are distorted in this fog and you can't tell which
is which but they moan pitch perfect and you
could score them to the tides, surf keeping
four-four time. Now and then the grace
notes of the gulls intrude.

The trawlers haul the bundled tourists
out to see the whales to make the payments
on the boat now that the banks are fished out.
And they are fished out. And in the winter
the local boys wrap alka-seltzer in soft bread
and feed the gulls to see them scavenge
and take off, glide and they explode as
the base hits the acid of the gut, raining
feathers, blood and meat. Rats with wings
they call them. Not beautiful. Not the birds,
nor boys, nor sea in this hard place.

THE RESCUE SWIMMER

The Coast Guard overflies the shore
today, the helo coming from the south
and you can predict where it will appear,
red and shiny as only government craft
can be, just over your roof peak, and
when you think they'll fly to Boston
over water, they veer north around
the point and head back down the cape.

Who might they be looking to save?
Anyone fool enough to be in May waters?
Aboard the craft are block and tackle,
bosun's chair and rescue swimmer: a plain
man who will hit the water in his dry
suit, blown up like a stuffed tick
to save someone from drowning.
Rescue Swimmer, with a light on his head

and guts beyond your ken. Misnamed,
he cannot swim but floats, and with luck,
catches what he's after,
or sometimes springs a leak
and sinks. Unlikely on a day like this—
his purview is December, swells like
hard peaks and cold you cannot bear.
When he's out there, pray for him.
In need or not. Pray.

III

EREBUS

Dark as, we say, that place on the edge of Ocean,
through which the shades all passed. But in
the Antarctic summer Mount Erebus shines pink.
The scientist, *ologist* of rock or ice, climbs
aboard the plane and keeps the mountain
in his view as they head out over the sea
to Christchurch and beyond.

                And I remember flying
out of Portland, Oregon, as St. Helens, Hood
and finally Rainier, that great ice cream cone
of a peak lay out like a toy landscape beneath us.
And don't we think that: *beneath us?*
Erebus named when Scott or Shackleton
or the helpless freezing crew knew what
Hell was in their poor canvas and wool.

Today we core the continent, *discover*
something else: that beneath two miles
of ice flows a river of mud and a volcano
burning, melting — earth doing what it does
despite us. Despite.

Kilauea

In the crevices of the new flow, green lichen
thrives on what would kill us.
Up slope, the eucalyptus are roman candles
and down here along the cliffs
we line up to watch the earth move.

Toward sunset you can hear the clicks and whirs
of cameras, and down below lava snaps and pops
as it hits the ocean in a red stream that floats
yards out to sea, then solidifies and sinks.

We crank the film out, as if what we take home
will let the others know: *We were there; we saw this.*
A Japanese tourist in pressed blue jeans elbows forward
to put his back to the flow and sea, just so.

And his wife, perfect white tennis shoes slipping
on the lava clinkers, stands to take this study in perspective.
We talk about our cameras. We wait for dark.
We are carving our names on the cliffs, drawing
on the walls of caves.

THE GERMAN IN THE SURF

is at least forty, maybe fifty, thin
and nearly bald, and a crescent of buttock
peeps from either side of his tiny paisley suit.
And his wife, or we assume his wife,
is no young thing — rolls of smooth fat
falling over her bikini bottom.

Over the roar we hear *Ja* and *schön.*

The camera is pressed to her face
framing him as he jumps and trips
into the water, now up to his chest.
And we can imagine back in Hamburg
or Darmstadt: *Look, there's Viktor*
in the surf. And on paper:
the endless blue Pacific and a speck —
which she waves to now. And he notices:
her noticing him, and amid
the noise, splash and cold, he waves
back, exuberant, twirling into the froth.

And it is, all of it, *schön:*

the man, the grown-up child, alight
with terror and with joy, flopping in the littoral
soup like something newly made.

Kahuku Flow, 1848

In March the earth shook for five days
and when April came it opened
and spewed lava. Those lucky enough
to be uphill watched as the flow engulfed
people, horses, cattle, then hit the ocean.
Then the sea roared back and took
the village. Cinder cones of green
grace the site now and a ranch sits
atop the flow: a spot with views of green
so ripe and fine it looks like Ireland
with all that blue around.

We imagine the dead,
like those of Pompeii, mummified,
under this smooth road, stopped with scythe
or rake in hand, a cow just looking up.
But that's not right; they ran,
saw it coming, and terrified, ran. Cows,
women, men, dogs, or those
at the beach, crouched behind a break
to miss the wave. The choice: to be boiled
by sea, cooked by flow itself.

There is nothing mammalian
beneath us. There's just that solid fire:
a`ā, pāhoehoe, lava's chunks and ropes
and nothing more.
Three hundred feet below lie
no fossils, relics, mummies. All
vaporized and all we know is what
the others saw — those uphill: families,
neighbors, friends: all grieving
and relieved.

Bahía

Outside Hermosillo, near the coast, Federales
formed a roadblock and what we norte-américanos see
are guns, guns over shoulders or across a back.
And young. Young Mayan faces and dark, deep-set eyes,

unreadable to us, ignorant gringos with barely a sentence
of Spanish amongst us. And we can't think of what to say
as we open the hatchback: *comidas*, food but cannot
remember the synonym for clothes. *Vêtements*? No!

That's French and we're not at any border.
Not bandits, the uniforms match and ammo is plentiful,
and we are going deep into Sonora and need to post

a bond, get a pass: *Solamente Sonora*. We promise we will
go no farther than the little fishing village where we'll eat
in the restaurant for almost nothing and be serenaded by
the handsome one-legged man who leads the mariachi band.

He's somewhere between forty and beyond and his trouser leg
is pinned up to his left thigh and where the leg went
we wonder. Accident? Fishing? Shark attack? He's graceful
on the crutches, even carrying the guitar. They sing. We pay.

Good American dollars in the musicians' hands. We're
supposed to pay in pesos and they're supposed to want them —
but the taxman isn't looking and a peso's worthless. Dinner
for five and a bottle of Cuervo in this exchange is twenty-

eight bucks. So, we overpay the musicians and the waiters
because we can. *Oblige, oblige* and there is nothing noble in it.
How much for a prosthesis? He could give up crutches
then. When we entered, we saw him sitting at the table,

crutches hidden by the wall and thought, *a handsome
man*. It was only when he rose in that one fluid motion that
we diminished him. We paid him extra out of pity
and were shamed.

SOUTH OF I-10

Just past the strawberry fields where it's at least a hundred
in the sun and migrants in trousers and long sleeves
stoop, bushel boxes balanced on one shoulder, the bus
drops its cargo on the beach. The children dance and hop
laying out their towels and lunch. There must be
fifty of them darting among six frantic teachers with whistles —
and if you pass, the wind carries the smell of childhood
sweat and milk.

      *

Toward San Onofre, cooling towers rise like two huge breasts
from the fog as if some destructive goddess lolled on the sand
up there, and road signs line the freeway: plain yellow squares
painted not with deer or tipping trucks but with running man,
woman, child — girl-child in a dress, pigtails flying. Imagine
the father with a suitcase, a doll trailing from the girl's hand,
her head turning. See it turning. The signs are for us, motorists
hauling ass at 70 or 80: *Here is where they cross.* At dawn.
Brake lights flash, and safe across they mass on the median
like frightened wildlife disturbed in their migration. Changing
shifts, *la migra* are loathe to chase them, fearing death themselves.
So they come: families, young boys, old men, crossing to the north
to catch a ride to Bakersfield, LA. Or not. Sometimes to be hit,
and crawling across four lanes, hit again. The color
of blood in any flag is red.

      *

At the beach, the day is calm, the water booms and roars.
Over the bluffs streak the fighters from a navy base, drowning
everything with their threat. They bank and roll
beautifully out to sea till lost finally in the depth of sky,
sound scoured by the surf — and the only thing left to hear
above it all are three small boys shrieking *fria, fria*
as they scramble from the ocean to the shore.

PLAY

The boy, Down's child, grinning face
hollowed like a dish, stands outside the stuccoed
building, playing in the parking lot where the cold
truck has backed up to the meat locker door.
It's what he's been waiting for all day, this
four-thirty-in-the-afternoon arrival
from the slaughterhouse in Hilo. And as
the headless, furless pigs run out
on the conveyor, the boy is beside himself.
He jumps and claps and pees his pants
as the driver hoists him up onto the dock
where he runs to hug the legs of a creature
that at this time yesterday was warm
and eating. And the boy's face
is so filled with joy, the sun seems to
stream from him, his jersey spotted
with water and blood as he hugs the pig's
legs, then the driver's. And now the driver
smooths the child's red hair, hoists him
down where he runs to the grass, throws
himself on his back and wings his arms
and legs as kids will do to make snow angels.
But it's eighty degrees here in February.
Paradise, they call it. And the parents
inside hum with effort, father stacks
the carcasses for morning cutting,
mother closing out the till. Soon they'll
take down the sign, shepherd the boy
into the car to head home for bath and sleep
and get ready, ready to do it all again tomorrow.

Band Concert at Hilo Bay

In this city where it rains two hundred seventy-eight
days a year, it's hot and sunny and the band is
playing Sousa, *The Last Days of Pompeii*,
here on the spot where a town used to be.
The conductor's face runs with sweat, black hair
and droplets flying as he instructs the flute to hold
and hold that last long note. And as the flute-sound ebbs,
the traffic stops, the light timed right so the note
soars out over Hilo Bay into the air and up
the palis, across the same water
that in 1960, earthquake warning clear,
the townsfolk descended on. Crowding the sea wall
to see the bay empty out, they ran out where
water had been to pick the fish flopping
in the muck.
Then the wave came in — drowning, smashing
like tinder the houses, stores, gas stations
of Shinmochi, where we've been sitting, the day
blue and hot, the flute note echoing,
the conductor bouncing on his toes,
and as we turn for our car the more expected
blares from the bandstand, a Sousa march,
brilliant and metallic, sending us across the street
in 4/4 time. And the conductor, bandleader
is grinning, grinning.

SOUTH POINT

Its trees bend horizontal, this
place the Polynesians came ashore.
Theory perhaps, but vestiges
of settlements remain. They came
in canoes. *Canoes*. And *written* history?
Europe — England, Norway, Spain,
Portugal were our "seafarers."

But Polynesians came across
four thousand miles of badly
named Pacific, came with breadfruit
trees and pigs, children and
house goods. Brought lives
with them to this land,
the first to heave to their horizon,

to find rich fishing, at this point,
where they tied their boats to cliffs,
(*pali* in their language), where still
you need to watch for holes —
if you go in here you're lost,
the fast track to Antarctica, the water
cold and shelfless. It's thirteen thousand

feet to bottom; and divers find no
wrecks, no wrecks on this island
where lava boils the cold Pacific.
And when they came, did mauka
clouds cover steaming cones?
The green hills signaling fresh water,
a place they could after all that distance
call home.

Punalu`u

Listen to the susurrus of the huge Pacific —
and the name the travelers gave this place:
Punalu`u, place of the fresh springs. The sky
is not white here but pale and perfect
and the sound and the kelpy smell will
calm you, calm. The sand, coarse and black
leaves the feet burning at midday but most
often we are here at dusk when the tourists
have gone and the palms gyrate and whisper
overhead, *surely, surely. Safe, safe* and
the turtles, having beached all afternoon
in sun, now lumber back to sea, the cove —
and the spray off the heiau melds with
the whale blow just offshore and the slap
of tail fin and pectoral. And we wander back
to the car as the sun heads west toward
Manila's evening, leaving us in peace.

THE DIVE

Below the surface, pushing at the ears
until the pain grows and one must rise to
equalize: establish pressure in and out,
the sea is filled. Here, we swim among the fish:
damsel, lion, barracuda — names we
give them as they go about their lives,
deep and oblivious to us.
Even the garden eels swaying like grass
at eighty feet won't care unless the big
ungainly creatures kick the sand.

And the diver ahead, his regulated breathing
smooth and even, waves his hands as if
to say *Come here; this way.* This is a spot
he knows. His hands look dead,
pale and white and wrinkled as they'd look
on the autopsy table, now moving in the current
like those of a drowned man.

The movement is voluntary yet too slow,
too deliberate to be that of his element.
And just below, a cleaner shrimp crawls
around the fish large enough to eat it.
Symbiotic: *You clean me and I won't eat you.
Not today.* And the diver's hands, like those
of a dancer, lead on to show us
what they've promised. Array of coral
and mantas gliding through our hair.

And when we ascend we do it slowly,
careful not to blow out lungs, bubble
with nitrogen, get bent. We break
the surface and spitting out the regulators,
breathe, speak. All the divers wondrous

at what they have seen:
that fish, that tube, that arch.

We are elated once again at being what we are.
Our little nod to danger left below
in being the strange, other, in a world
ignorant and dismissive of us, a world
in which we cannot do the simplest
human thing: breathe.

The Century Plant

Agave. Gray-green plant whose leaves
if they can be called that, not swords or bayonets,
fling themselves up and out. Plant them
beneath your window to keep the burglars away:
a roofer, falling in a copse, grove, bunch
of them, spent three months in critical
care — the things passed right through him.
Oh but we love them, love a plant because it grows
huge and strong, because it shoots up blossoms
phallic and thick as tree trunks, but most
because its life span, we like to think,
mimics ours.
                    It blooms. It dies.
Then we have the backhoe come and dig
the damned thing up. An American plant, spending
itself in the theatrical gesture of bloom. *Look,*
we say, *a baby.* A small agave has sprouted from
the seed of the dead. It's as big as a dinner plate.
It will outlive us.

Lō`ihi

Fifteen hundred feet up and nine miles in
we can smell the ocean today.
And out there it's blue glass, pacific,
kind — as if you'd bob in place
and the currents out past the point
wouldn't take you to the nearest
and next continent: Antarctica.
Huge and blue and smelling not
of death and brine as the Atlantic does,
but of enormity and of the whale breaching
off the point last night, immune
to currents — breeding in the frigid waters
off Alaska, feeding and birthing here.
She makes us draw our breath — or lose it.
And miles out there, an island forms,
boils three thousand feet down:
Lō`ihi, named before its birth by
a species that may well kill itself
before the new land bursts, heaves,
makes its way to air. Ten thousand
years we give this island we have named
before it lurches from the sea, graceful
and enormous and unaccountable
for what we call it: land, whale
volcano ... *our* earth.

TRADES

It's blowing thirty mph today with gusts to forty
and you can imagine George Vancouver,
William Bligh and Cook under full sail to bring
mosquitoes, pox and weeds across ten thousand
miles of ocean to paradise and fast. Always land.

I sit on my acre surrounded by big land owned
by big money, land stolen from the natives
who took it too, landed and said *ours*.
With their pigs and fowl and crops
to decimate the forest, said *ours*.
And the white sails and frigates and me
with my little car arriving on the barge.

Across the continent: Cleveland, Milwaukee,
Oacoma, South Dakota and then across
the ocean to this land which will outlive us
all and our transport: paddles, sails, barges
cars. Cement and steel will crumble and
the land will be the land again, green
and black. Ocean eaten and volcano made,
it will outlast us and our descendants.
To the ants on the table and the roaches
under the gas tank shall we will it.

IV

Equinox, New York

On the pedestrian mall, in the city of a man whose bed
you stayed in, stretched out in, wallowed in for weeks,
you imagine he could walk through that door there,
the jeweler's door, looking for a gift for wife or daughter —
and even though you know he is three thousand miles away,
you see him fingering amethyst or emerald ...

Though you hate the domestic in a lover,
the way, years ago, even the sight of a man's hands
could kill your desire cold. You loved the rough play
of muscles in the forearm. Now the hands intrigue you:
the too-long little fingernail tracing a red line up your leg
because you'd bitten and he thought you liked pain.

Which is the hammer and which the anvil?

Now you are nearly happy to know you are on his ground, a spy.
These green hills going to fall, your memory is virulent;
you catch it like a flu, nurse it. Melancholy snuggles up
and gives more comfort than any human presence might.
Remember the spot of blood on the nightgown, the whiff of *Fracas,*
a snatch of Mingus from a window.

He won't come through that door, his slow amble promising
the slow trace of lips on your belly.
You're safe to make the fiction of your life,
to love the one you love the most: your want, your longing.

TRAIN

It's shirt-sleeve weather in November, a day so extraordinary that the neighbors are walking out their doors with their mouths open as if to suck in this uncanny air and keep it for the winter. We want to enjoy the day, every minute, but we talk or work and do not, do not attend. And how can we? How is it done, this attending to what is present and passing all at once?

Tonight we'll be able to lie with the windows open and if the wind is right, around midnight we'll hear the train as it passes up the valley — as it did the summer nights its whistle called us to the geographic cure: another time, another day, another continent perhaps and life would be better, lovers happier, the dead un-dead.

One night outside Trenton, our train crossed the black water of the Delaware and a man staggered out of a bar pushing a woman; in the seconds it took for us to pass, he knocked her down, pointed a gun, a hard extension of the hand we could imagine he'd used on her before, and she flew back at the Dolphin Room, shattering the glass door as he slid into the dark.

Passing at a hundred mph we saw what we saw or dreamed we saw, no time to drop our jaws, rise from our seats, open the windows and scream, a sound that would be drowned in the metal slipstream of the train.

Here with the windows open, in the warm metallic dark, in the desk across the room a cheap watch ticks off hours and has for two years since, half a continent away, under a railroad bridge, a man in a soiled baseball cap and layers of clothes, a brown paper bag under his arm, spoke into my window.

His face was falling, not what we describe when we mean disappointed, but falling, his cheeks pouches and under his eyes bags like liquid and the eyes hidden, so gray as to be colorless. And he wanted to sell his watch. He was trying to *catch a train, get a bite to eat.*

I had a watch so I offered him five bucks. *I'm not like that*, he said and as he pulled the watch from his wrist I caught a whiff of alcohol, not beer on the breath but the aura that comes from years of wine or vodka, although if I'd had a case in the back seat he wouldn't have taken it, fouled our transaction like that.

As I pulled away I saw him receding in the mirror, crossing to the rail yard through the mesquite, falling on his hands and knees in the road, the bag spilling into traffic and him leaning, pulling it toward him, slowly straightening his hat and his body as I rounded the corner and lost sight.

A long train came out of the yard, gaining speed, six engines and the cars: Hanjin, Evergreen, Sea Land came alongside before they veered off into the creosote toward El Paso. The whistle sang into the canyon even though there's no crossing up there.

I drove east wearing two watches. Now the plate is rubbed off the bezel to reveal dull steel and if we held it close tonight we could see that even though it's November the date reads July, could hear it ticking, still keeping good time.

NIGHT FISHING
for CG

A bilious moon skewered on the end of the jetty
and bass jumping shiny as dimes are what he leans towards,
these nights he can't sleep. As he rocks, casting
into the surf, his old tennis shoes
suck and drag, and as his shorts slide
along his thighs, the shrapnel furrows are bled white
and harmless in the moonlight. I want to put my lips
on them, my wet fingers. But what I do is take the hooks
from the fish, too small this July to be keepers.
I slide the barbs out for him, holding the hook up
so he can see it in the moon's path,
and then I let them go, and they pour themselves
out of my hands, slowly, back to their own element.

Karmic

Another withdrawal from the Karma Bank as the fly
I've slapped falls from my thigh and the welt raises.

Who is it I have killed today, and what done to
come back a maggot on the compost pile, or the old

dog lying in the grass snoring who will also go
soon enough? And *my* actions? The waiter

whose math error would have cost him twenty bucks
had I not been honest, the beaver we tried to lift from

the dam sump? A good day's work is only that. Is
it the bee I hear or the doppler of the motorbike out

on the highway? My friend, who grew up by the inter-
state, whose house is gone now, torn down for road

and industry, swears the highway in deep night sounds
of soprano voices. Dido on her terrace singing to her end,

"Remember me but, ah! Forget my fate." And the ravens
circle the pond, cawing in this moment of quiet

from the highway. Now they've gone, too. We and Dido,
those of us left keep calling, calling our own refrain.

SMALL SONG

The lilacs shiver in the oncoming
thunderstorm. Now the grass becomes
a jungle thanks to twelve days' rain.
And we can't mow or weed or do
the things we do to make this home.
From the house, in the background,
a mandolin, a reggae tune in counter-
point to the evening grosbeak I can't see
in these new leaves; I only hear him
going like a robin on amphetamines.
What I've got here is this day. Hours
of daylight left on this twenty-fifth
of May in this ongoing year. Year in
and out and past my death and yours
this planet spins until its sun burns out
and dark comes down for good. But
now the cat in this lap is warm, the
mandolin sweet and the downbeat
hangs with thunder in the air.

Just June

The black fly trying to crawl up my nose is
perhaps the offspring of the offspring

of the offspring that left a welt on my neck
last week. Isn't their life-span two days,

mouthless and sexed because *that* is their
business? And if they have no mouths,

what are these welts? And what do I
seem to them except a heap of welcome

warmth or blood. And the next day,
in the same chair, is that a grand-bug

trying to crawl under the lens of my
shades? The vitreous call of the eye

or merely bumble? It's June at last,
the cherries are in bloom and thunder

rumbles down the landscape and still
these damned flies will not give up and die.

May flies they are called, and for a reason.
Don't they know we're two days into June?

THE RACER

Monopolizing the left lane, pacing the wet floor,
bare feet slapping the tile, he is obsessed.
As the young woman in the water paddles
feet only then breaks to a crawl at his word,

he looks at nothing but his watch, the feet,
the arms, the turn like a seal's and he sees
none of us, not even the retarded man who
yowls with joy and claps as his helper works

to get his shoes on tight. He's hooting at the sky
when the sun breaks through the atrium and he
points to the light on water. And on the other
side, the clock runs down on the girl who is

in her twentieth lap now. Her sinewy body
is slick, her cap glows green in the sun;
we can't see her eyes behind her goggles
and she's intent on the coach and where he's

taking her. The old woman climbing out after
aerobics looks at them too; there seems to be no joy
in what they do — never looking past each other
and the clock. The rest of us are out now, to

the showers, lockers, and in the sauna, slick
and wet with chlorine, my ass leaves a print
on the wooden bench like a truffle or a thyroid,
two-lobed shadow and when I put my tongue

on the back of my hand in the hundred twenty
degree heat, I taste salt. My heart pumps in
my ears, my skin bright and salty from
the exercise and heat. Later, flushed,

wrung out, passing to the cold outdoors
I hear the coach still yelling "no" and
"more" and "there, there" as if they'd
both arrived somewhere.

ECLIPSE

In memory of Lou Van Hoosear, MD

The yard shone blue, air the color
of cold and by then he'd gone into coma.
Well enough to see the daffodils a week before,
the Vermont hillside yellow from a half-mile off,
he gripped the seat all the way home, along the rough
dirt roads where they had to stop every three miles,
not to rest, the way an old man walking might,
but for morphine. And then he'd slept three days.

But he'd seen the flowers, which, on the day
of the eclipse seemed green — a child's
primary color lesson: *yellow and blue make green* —
in this air of a color not to be believed
and the trees casting all those shadows
— at least two for every branch —
which, at full eclipse, stood still in an air so cold
and perfect we could imagine that's how it would look
when our own sun began to burn away, not the pale
lemon disk of winter sitting with promise on the horizon,
but here, in spring, high in the sky — and dark.

By late May he was dead, the flag snapped in the breeze,
the picture of the eighteen wheeler still hung
on the bathroom wall. The thing he'd give up medicine
for: the long haul, across the desert in a Kenworth.
Like the ones coming up now, a year later,
out of the San Pedro valley and into the sun toward
Tucson, the truckers with their sleeves rolled
to their armpits revealing the sleek meat of triceps,
the part the cannibals call choice.

Today, out on I-10, a train came along beside
the road, and all the way up the valley, till the track
split off into the canyon, into the creosote and mesquite,
it kept pace at seventy and headed out into the sun over
California, over Samoa.

New Hampshire

She's standing belly to the bridge rail, sun just cresting
the mountain to the east, redwing blackbirds soaring under her,
and her hair is lifted by the west wind and the slipstream
of cars passing at seventy.

There's no story to tell you here: how she misses
the husband's smooth body on hers, the way he looked going down
into the pile of leaves last fall, heart blown out
and the rake in his hand upright like a pikestaff.

There's just the bridge, and a hundred feet down, the river,
shallow and cold; and the spot where the divers
have just dredged the body of the trucker who went in last
December, headfirst through the windshield, then the ice.

She will be able to tell what he won't: the lips blown open,
every inch of skin on fire, waking up at all. Six months
of hospital and she will walk to the bank, shovel snow, even
have a lover whose glance dissolves her between knees and sternum.

But nothing is like these seconds: that wind in her ears,
the heat, the desire of the arrow for the target.

Seeking the Grave of Albert Camus

Freedom is the right not to lie. —Camus

We have five days and I need, want, to spend one looking
for the grave. On the tiny winding roads into the Luberon,

over the mountains, through the little town of Jouques, we
find the village and drive round it twice looking for

the *cimetière*. Are these the roads? Was it one of these he died
on in a '49 Ford or Mercury, a car my father had, its head-

lights slitted eyes in an evil face? Or was that James Dean?
Have I conflated deaths and cars? I remember the car

looking crumbled, partly crushed on a country road.
And the history says he was driven — yet I recall

he drove. The old, grainy black & white photos, a body
falling from the car. Would he have lived had

he been driving? The snaky roads and narrow, the dark,
drizzle, the rain-soaked pavement in the headlamps. And

he'd be dead now anyway, wouldn't he? Of age or cigarettes or
some other misfortune. On that night — no perfect Provençal

sky as we have now, searching through the little cemetery.
And the grave is there like so many other graves and

bending down to sweep the vegetation from the head
stone, the scent that rises to my face is herbal. I pick a sprig

and crush it in my hands: rosemary, best marinade
for fish here in Provence. Because of myth and meaning

I pick a bunch to take away. Rosemary: for remembrance.

CHANSON DE PROVENCE

Oh, let me, Purcell's plaint echoes
through the house, in front
of this, Cézanne's mountain, although
not his view, the green, lower slopes
reforested after all these years. The air
flowing out is *the last song Mr. Purcell wrote,*
it being in his sickness. And did he see France,
this view, this mountain? The countertenor's voice
on the October air reminds us that at home,
in America, our house is just coming awake
and far west it is the hour of low ebb,
the hour when the old and sick give out,
give in and go. And beyond this mountain
the Etang de Berre is dead, the Mediterranean
fished out, and the scrim of air lying
over the Carmargue, even in a terrific
wind, stinks. Still, the voice hollows
the old rock, the sun, the fleece of cloud
over the mountain. *Come Heavy Sleep*
rolls out the window now,
down the hill, over the bare rock
of Provence, and dissipates towards the sea.

Summer Poem

Feed the birds, tie up the peony
and mow the lawn. Now
the earth takes another
pass around the sun. And it is
summer. We're tilting northward
now, tilting and the dogs roll and
the grass and food grow and
the cats chase the birds on
the other side of the glass. And yes,
today is cool and windy and
the pond is filled with cat's paws
and trout. Another day. Perfect
day. And gone.

The Copulation of Lepidoptera

On my deck this hot last day in January, the Pacific out there
endless, boundless, and these two Monarchs undistinguished
by color flap and twist in sun shade, sun shade, as if we who
stand over them are part of the surrounding trees. Twist in
the ritual of what humans always compare to combat. And they
take off — one above, one below, flitting as Lepidoptera do,
over the small pandanus tree, and then he, or maybe it is she
for all we know of the breeding of the butterfly, lets go —
To make cocoon or tent? They do what they do:
Lepidoptera, Hymenoptera, birds ... and what
they do is eat, breed and pass on their genetic information.
That they fly five thousand miles and over water, on the trades
does not speak courage. It's just nature.

Or in Vermont in May, every species copulating, the beavers
at the dam, the canadas, and butterfly chases butterfly down
the middle of the gravel road. Oh, and aren't they blissful, all
dip and glide and we can hear a half mile away the diesel
downshift as he hits the hill. He's coming sure and fast and
they have lighted one atop the other, all wings beat slow
and languid and oblivious as the truck roars over them,
dust and pollen and wings scattered into the dust cloud
above the pond. And they've survived that cyclone, the two
of them as one as they maneuver to the gatepost, then
disengage. They've done what they set out to do and now
one heads south over the pond and the other floats and
bats among the lilacs, usual and miraculous.

The Genitive Case

Valete discupli! Imperative! She cries,
swinging her arm like an orator. First Period
Latin and she's on one knee and now
a senior has to help her up because
it's nine o'clock and she's been into the vodka already.
She keeps it in the teachers' room, in the closets
of her one bedroom. She's sixty and her gray
curls are tight from yesterday's appointment.
She's retiring next year.
                              But the lesson for today
is the genitive case and on her feet she recites
whole passages of Virgil, passages heavy with
the case in question: *the field of the farmer,*
the wife of the farmer, the daughter of the farmer,
slave of. And in one word.

Now, in this cold April, in Vermont, the stranger
has returned from a walk past the graveyard
and he's entranced by the stones. *1863, so old.*
He relates inscriptions, reading from a lined notepad:

Brown
Sarah, wife of Asa
Lucy, daughter of

So brief, he says, *so brief.*

PEAK

The most beautiful tree this October twelfth
graces the lawn of the funeral parlor and in
a week it will be bare while others hold
their leaves. Gorgeous, all right, brief
and ironic standing where and as it does.

And we two friends drive by saying *Oh, yes*
it peaked on the sixth at my house and on
the ninth at hers. Peak. We await it, excited
at the top of the roller coaster, on the sidewalk
before the mansard-roofed funeral home.

We know it is attained when it
has passed and not until. Are we
two women at our peak, she turned
fifty this year, her beauty pale and
stark as it has been always.

And on the lawn the men come out this Saturday
to greet the mourners, slick and somber and unctuous
in their black suits and making a racket as they
kick through crimson, gold and palomino leaves,
the leavings of the tree now peaked.

CRICKET IN THE FILE DRAWER

He must be living on dust bunnies back there.
It's September and he's singing for
the female who is not here but outside, she
who might respond to lifted wings.

Not a visual girl, she'd get the smell;
the goo secreted beneath those
wings is what draws her. But in the grass,
yards away, she has no idea her dreamboat's

there beyond the wall. Behind the files
for "charity," "cars" and "veterinary
expense," he's frantic, safe from the frost
that will kill his kin, and from the office cat.

He's off on another riff, lifting
his wings in hope and singing as
the sun heads south, the air's sweet
gauze and in the top of the birch,

the goldfinch is a yellow din. Here
in the long last light of September
there's nothing but song.

Solstice

On the first full day of summer the sun is up
the sky as far as it will get and now it will
head south to warm the Antipodes, where today
it rains and gales blow up from the Antarctic.

Here it is summer already, the lawn mowed, garden
weeded and nostalgia for summers past makes her
way into this place. The years of WWII bunkers
on South Beach and the tar coating our feet from

the boats out there and green-eyed Billy, now gone to
fat and trouble, trying to pull me through his bedroom
window. Now, Lily Briscoe paints the lighthouse again,
and my cousins run across the yard. And the others, all

of them. Grown middle-aged... or dead or sick and
their children, for Christ's sake, all grown up.
We were something. The great bonfire on the beach
and sex in the dunes with someone I would

never see or taste again, and hanging on each
other before the fire. The other years: crossing
the Tyrrhenian Sea in a summer storm, fearing
the boat will sink because they have, they do.

Below decks everyone pukes and prays to *Dio,
Deo, Allah*, so I go above and lash my sleeping
bag to the deck rail and wedged between
the bulkhead and two steel rods, I sleep. Nothing

between me and the wild ocean but a clothesline
rope. And awake as we chug into Brindisi, all
of us repeating *grazie, grazie* as we disembark to live
another summer. Now, all these years on, we

see another summer coming, relentless in
its blooms and breeze and thunder rolling up
the valley and apple blossoms strewn like snow
flakes on the ground.

Owl

He's on the wire, across the road in the February
late-day fog, the days now lengthening and the trees
at the edge of the field all but invisible and the temp
at fifty farenheit with a promise of spring that won't

come for three months yet; and in the yard now the last
of our guinea fowl squawks and owl sits in the cherry
tree, the wind gone still. It's a Snowy, stoic and solitary
and he watches the foolish human, barefoot in the foot-

and-a-half of snow and the .22 hoisted to her shoulder.
The snow is mid-way to her knees and sighting down
the barrel she shoots wide, wild and purposely
and the owl retreats across the road watching as

the stupid guinea stands in the yard and
will not be caught, runs from the human who can't
grab anything but a handful of purple feathers for her
trouble. The guinea and her cohorts refused to be stationed

in the chicken house all winter, safe for duration of
the hard months, fed and warm in with the laying hens.
And now, now she's all that's left. And owl
sits. He's patient and looks down as if to say: *You*

will not shoot an owl. And he's right.
Bad luck, at least, and truth to tell we welcome him,
his solitary grace. Later, as dusk comes on and nothing
is discernible among the trees, up close on

the west side of the house, feathers litter snow and
delicate droplets form a map, a trail to where owl
stands over his kill, a body now, and stares in
the window at the woman, the world all shades of

gray — sky, fog, owl, snow — the lavender
feathers of the guinea the only disturbance in our
world, and red melting into snow.

On the Mill Race

A pair of great blue herons in the dead cherry last night
and as dusk came on in rain and sleet,
the wail of a loon sailed across the pond
out from among the canadas, mergansers and a grebe or two.
Here in the lilacs, not three feet from my window,
a ruby-crowned kinglet, then another
and a yellow shafted flicker on our lawn —
the lawn that once belonged to MacNighter
and before that Fletcher — and our old cats
buried out there beneath this spring's mud.

Where the old barn stood, where the soil is good from
years of pigs and cattle, where the brown mutt followed
MacNighter to the barn in a spring blizzard
to watch over the early calf in the stall, warm and steamy
of a March night. And on the overturned bucket
by the door, the old man stroked the yellow tiger,
as on the back porch we built years later, I stroked
the black-and-white who would go missing
that next winter, but this night purred
as the August Perseids fell down
and tanks filled the streets of Moscow.

And MacNighter and Fletcher and those before —
the orange cat, the boy lost in Belgium and another
in the next war. The spring hopeful with calves,
the milk hitting the bucket with a ping
and in the milk can's top, warm liquid for the cat
and the purr filling the barn.

Or August, here, years later with the cat
and the peepers and the bullfrogs and the voice
calling from the lighted house: "Where are you?"
And "Come in."

Ellen Dudley is the author of *Slow Burn* (Provincetown Arts Press, 1997). She is the recipient of a Vermont Council on the Arts Fellowship as well as fellowships to the Dorland Mountain Arts Colony and the Vermont Studio Center. She is founding editor/publisher of the *Marlboro Review*. She lives in Marlboro, Vermont, where she is a partner in a construction company.